25 THINGS THAT _REALLY_ MATTER IN LIFE

A Little Book, With a Big Message

Gary A. Johnson

COURTLAND PRESS

Courtland Press
6503 Old Branch Avenue
Suite 202
Temple Hills, Maryland 20748-2645

ATTENTION CORPORATIONS, UNIVERSITIES, COLLEGES, AND
PROFESSIONAL ORGANIZATIONS: Quantity discounts are available on
bulk purchases of this book for educational and gift purposes, or as premiums
for increasing magazine subscriptions or renewals. These discounts are
also available to various Book Clubs. Contact Courtland Press for more
information.

ISBN-10: 0-9791113-0-7
ISBN-13: 978-0-9791113-0-3

Visit our Web site at www.25ThingsThatReallyMatterInLife.com.
Visit our blog at www.25things.wordpress.com.

Cover and Interior Designed by
The Writer's Assistant
www.thewritersassistant.com

DEDICATION

I would like to dedicate this book to the following people:

My mother, Ernestine G. Johnson, and my father, Samuel H. Johnson. I am as proud of you as you are of me.

My sister, Judy, who has her own story to tell but will never put it on paper.

My uncle Fred Smith, who is more like a brother. You consistently reach out and share life lessons with me for the sole purpose of making me a better father. Thank you.

To Anthony and Christopher for reasons too numerous to mention.

To the memory of my late grandparents Solomon and Ethel Gary. Grandma, I still have your original letters and read them often for inspiration.

Lastly, I would like to dedicate this book to every person who has an idea, a vision or a dream.

ACKNOWLEDGMENTS

Thank you, Deborah. Your support made it possible for me to take risks with my businesses. Years from now, our sons will have wonderful memories because they grew up with a stay-at-home dad. Make no mistake, you made it possible.

To my dear friend, Patricia Waddell: you epitomize many of the things that *really* matter in life. Outside of my mother, you were the first woman to stand up to me. I didn't like it and you didn't care. Who knew we would continue to be friends for over thirty years?

I would like to acknowledge Tammy Richards Le-Sure of Richards Public Relations, who was relentless in her pursuit for me to share my experiences in the form of a book. Tammy was not the only person to encourage me to write a book, but she was the most persuasive. Gloria White (a woman I met on the subway) and columnist Mike Ramey consistently urged me to finish the book. Thank you.

I would also like to acknowledge author and publisher Jessica Tilles of Xpress Yourself Publishing for serving as my consultant. Thank you, Jessica, for your willingness to share your knowledge with me. People like you are few and far between.

Stacée L. Hardiman, working with you helped me reshape my reality about single working mothers. Thanks for allowing me to be a part of your world.

Thank you Carla Scopeletis for reviewing my manuscript and helping me make my thoughts clear.

Last but not least, thank you Floyd Dickens, Jr. and Jacqueline B. Dickens. Attending your seminar motivated me to quit my job and become a consultant. You "adopted" me, mentored me, and literally made me a part of your family. I hope I'm representing the family well.

CONTENTS

INTRODUCTION

INTRODUCTION

We live in a very fast-paced society. It seems as if almost everything is designed to happen as quickly as possible. We don't need cash these days; we just "swipe and go." We don't have to stop and pay our toll. We simply flash a card and keep rolling. We have drive-thru windows for doughnuts and coffee. We have a generation of children who put food in the microwave oven, watch it turn, and yell, "hurry!" If you are one of those folks who have to have it "now," then this book was written for you.

25 Things That Really Matter In Life is designed to get you started living a better life within the next fifteen minutes. Moreover, here's the best thing: You can read this book in an hour and it will still be relevant five years from now. The book changes with you. If you're looking for a book written by a highly credentialed author with letters after his name to help you find out who you are and what happened in your life that made you the way you are, this is not the book for you. If you want a book to help you begin to change your life _right now,_ then keep reading, because this _is_ the book for you. _25 Things That Really Matter In Life_ was written for people who have some sense of what they need to do to change their lives, but don't quite know how to go about doing it.

I wrote this book at one of the lowest points in my life. My businesses were heavily in debt and, although I continued to function every day, there were times when I did not feel good about myself. Through it all, I continued to try to affect the lives of others through my training seminars and speeches. I also went out of my way to make sure I was an active dad for my sons.

At times, I think I showed symptoms of depression. I never sought a medical opinion, but I had many of the signs. My weight fluctuated, I became reclusive, I stopped communicating to some of the people close to me, and I did not open my mail for weeks. There were days when I would wake up with no sense of purpose. Intellectually, I knew I should be doing certain things, but I could not get myself to take action. This was unusual for me, because I'd always been an "action-oriented" person who lived with a clear sense of purpose.

Throughout this period, I never stopped trying to be better. I always felt I would bounce back and find my way.

I knew I was not living my best life, because I did not own it. I desperately tried to be the person who was accessible to everyone, the person who always had a minute for one and all. I was not prepared to deal with those who wanted to use me for their own good. People who weren't close to me nonetheless thought nothing of calling me at home and asking for favors or other preferential treatment. Some would even ask for money. There were times when I felt overwhelmed by the responsibilities that seemed to be taking over my life. I could feel myself withdrawing from some people and just wanting to be alone.

As the pressure mounted, it was easier for me to push everyone away, suppress my feelings and endure the stress, rather than talking about my problems with someone who might be able to help me. The only time I did not withdraw was when I was around my children. I actually looked forward to being with them; getting involved in their world kept me out of mine. Their world was fun. At the end of the day, I was still dad, and I always seemed to make things better for them.

What was I missing? What did I need? I grew up in a loving two-parent household, with a large and loving extended family: grandparents, cousins, uncles, aunts and neighbors. I was never abused in any way. And I was surrounded by people who loved me. Yet, as I grew older, I began to question if I ever felt loved. Feeling isolated will do that. It's not rational, but it seemed real at the time.

On a Friday night, in September 2006, I decided to write down the things that *really* mattered to me. I stopped the list at twenty-five. Putting pen to paper was a measure of accountability. I was ready to be accountable and make a change in my life. Writing my thoughts on paper was therapeutic and gave me a sense of relief. This process was a "freeing" experience that helped me to feel good again.

25 Things That Really Matter In Life is a little book with a big message. The techniques and steps that I describe in the following pages are ones that I've been using for over thirty years. If you commit to them, I guarantee you will live a more meaningful and healthier life. By design, this book is simple and easy to use. There are three major steps to living a better life:

- Step 1: Read *25 Things That Really Matter In Life*.

- Step 2: List *25 Things That You Really Want To Do In Life*.

- Step 3: Life Mastery —Living your best life.

The first step is to study *25 Things That Really Matter In Life* and make them a part of your daily life. Visualize yourself being *successful,* so when negative circumstances present themselves, *25 Things That Really Matter In Life* will automatically counter the negative with positive affirmations. If you do this, I *guarantee* you will be successful, however you define success, and you will receive all of the gifts life has for you.

Changing certain aspects of your life is not easy. Looking at your life and the choices you've made in an open and honest way can be an emotional and gut-wrenching experience. As you rewind your mental tapes, you are likely to see a pattern of decision making that is self-defeating or sabotaging. It doesn't have to be that way. This is your chance to enhance your quality of life and to feel good about yourself. You can improve your situation today. Don't blow this opportunity. Victory is near.

How did I turn the *negative* aspects of my life into something *positive?* First, I acknowledged I was not in control of some aspects of my life. Many of the decisions I made for my life were sound and reasonable. So what went wrong? I did not know how to *execute* those decisions properly.

25 Things That Really Matter In Life taught me to think *strategically* about the personal aspects of my life. There was a period in my life when I consistently made bad decisions and excuses for my actions when things did not go my way. Self-accountability improved my situation. Improving your life is not about *luck;* it's about *hard work and effective effort.* Most of my barriers were self imposed, which is likely to be the case with you. If you're not willing to do the hard work and look inside yourself, close this book! You are not ready.

The principles in this book will help you create a flexible and customized plan for your life. My customized plan consists of the 3 C's: Commitment, Communication, and Consistency. I made a personal commitment to change aspects of my life. I learned to communicate openly and honestly with myself. This was difficult because it required me to change my mindset and not listen to the "mental Muzak" that caused me to do stupid things. Last, but not least, I realized my new behavior would work only if I consistently used one or more of the principles every day.

In this book, I list the 25 things that really matter in my life. I also share how the 25 things that influenced _my_ life can help you improve _yours._ You can control the quality of your life by making _25 Things That Really Matter In Life_ a part of your daily living. Once you have "mastered" them, I will show you how to start _living your best life._

When you read the words in this book, know that I am not speaking from an exalted position. This is what I've experienced and know to be true. My job is to tell you everything I know to help you make your life successful. Your job is to take what I tell you and develop a flexible and customized plan that will work for you. If you make a commitment to do this, you can live every day as if it's your last, and enjoy your life. If you want to change your life, change the way you act and the way you think.

Let's get started!

STEP 1

STEP 1

25 THINGS THAT *REALLY* MATTER IN LIFE

1. Faith

Have faith in God or believe in something other than yourself. Faith is the greatest power at your disposal. Faith never fails. You need to believe in yourself in order to convince others to believe in you. Pray and ask God to give you the strength and humility to be more focused and forgiving. Leave the negative aspects of living to a higher power so you can live your best life. The only time you can fail is when you give up on faith, so incorporate faith as part of your spirit. Then, when negative circumstances confront you, you automatically go into "Faith Mode," a way of life that allows you to behave without fear of the opposing forces that may surround you. There are levels of faith. Having strong faith is a process. If your faith is not at the highest level, you may suffer a setback. This is no reason to quit or give up. You will not be strong overnight. *(Faith moved me to quit my job. With a wife and two small children, I chose to change my career and pursue a path I had been doing* _for less than three years. I developed a solid and flexible plan that guided me to where I am today. There are no limitations on how much faith you can have. Fear causes paralysis. Faith is an energizer.)_

2. Family

Spending quality time with your family (spouse, children, and parents) can extend your life. Loved ones at home, who love you, are among the things in life that _really_ matter. _(When I was growing up, family was important in my life. Aunts, uncles and cousins lived in my neighborhood. Most of us worshipped at the same church and vacationed together. Family was a way of life that was never challenged. That foundation remains solid today. In past years, I've distanced myself from some aspects of my family, but my family never distanced themselves from me.)_

3. Love

Despite the high divorce rate (approximately fifty percent), studies show people who are in committed, monogamous relationships believe they have healthier and happier lives. A strong emotional connection with the one you love is paramount for a happy existence. Love should feel euphoric. When you find that special someone who will not take advantage of your vulnerabilities, who you trust implicitly, who can communicate with you in a manner that is "hearable" and who is consistent in his or her behavior, then you will live a happier and more meaningful life. When you totally surrender to the other person, you will experience a bond sealed by a higher power. One of the best things about having a true love is that everything you do together is special. *(Love is expressed in many ways: patience, kindness, caring, forgiveness, and so forth. Self-love is probably the most important aspect of love. I've learned that you must have boundaries in love. You can't keep saying "Yes" without being able to say "No." Falling in love is easy. Maintaining love is something entirely different. In my early relationships, I was comfortable with conflict (arguing.) Later in life, I overcompensated by avoiding conflict. I'm a "work in progress" when it comes to having my needs met. For me, loving someone and making someone feel loved are different. Love requires balance. Are you able to identify the important components of love and balance them with the other aspects of your life? Some of us confuse lust with love. Lust desires to take . . . love desires to give. Some people confuse control for love. If you say "no" and your partner hears "let's negotiate," you're in a potentially toxic relationship.)*

4. Children

A happy family is the key to a happy life, especially with your children. Quality relationships with your children will help you stay balanced and will help them lead balanced lives. The only way to cultivate and sustain solid relationships with your children is to spend quality time with them. Turn off the television, leave work early, and invest your time where you'll get the most return, which is with the ones you love. From the time my children were infants, I took them everywhere I went. I even set up a workstation at my office and home office for them. We worked, laughed, talked and played every day. One of my fondest memories is watching my children laugh. When children are laughing, all is right with the world. *(I was born to be a dad. Having a good relationship with my children is one of the most important factors for my happiness and stability. The best gift that a man can give to his children, in addition to spending time with them, is to model the appropriate behavior consistently.)*

5. Good Health

Good health is paramount to good living. Good health is something many people tend to appreciate only when it's deteriorating or gone. You can have millions of dollars in the bank, a beautiful house and a nice car, and it will mean very little if you're sick. Take care of your mind, body and soul. *(I'm in relatively good health. I have no physical limitations. Like many people, living a healthy life style was not a priority. Although I never smoked, used drugs, or drank alcohol, I had poor eating habits and didn't exercise consistently throughout the first half of my life. I wish I had acted differently. Today, I realize that those poor eating habits have not been kind to me. Living a healthier lifestyle can add years to your life.)*

6. Peace of Mind

There is nothing so comforting as having peace of mind. It is strongly connected to having control over your life. Learn to breathe properly, slow down, and focus on the good things of life. Achieving this kind of peace also allows you to choose how you spend your time. *(Having peace of mind is one of the best-kept secrets to success. With it, anything seems possible.)*

7. Adequate Rest

Experts say the majority of us do not get enough sleep. Less sleep means added stress. Our bodies need time to recover. If you follow *25 Things That <u>Really</u> Matter In Life,* you will have the luxury of long, uninterrupted hours of rest. *(There are times when I do not get enough rest. I consistently push my body and function at less than full capacity. But I know that everything gets better with rest.)*

8. Giving

When you give from the heart, good things will happen to you. Throughout my adult life, I gave my time, money and attention to those who were in need. I gave unconditionally. I did not ask or expect anything in return. Give to leave a legacy. Consider establishing a family foundation that will carry out your wishes and have a positive impact on others long after you're gone. There is no greater satisfaction than giving. *(I have a history of giving selflessly to others. True giving feels good. I never give out of guilt. I give because I want to and because I can. I have never regretted giving.)*

9. Dreams and Passions

If you have a dream and you pursue it with passion, you will surpass all boundaries of thought and imagination. I used to dream about one day being paid for doing something I enjoyed so much that I would gladly do it for free! My dream came true, and I've been living my dream since 1995, when I quit my job and stepped out on faith to start my businesses. I love what I do. I work harder and longer than I did when I had a job.

Following my dream is, for me, truly a labor of love. Never lose your ability to dream. If you can *see* it, you can *be* it. *(I believe in dreams and I believe in passion. The combination of the two is awesome and euphoric for me. Living with or being surrounded by people who don't share your dreams is a potential obstacle to your personal development. I was fortunate to be surrounded by people who supported my dreams.)*

10. Wealth

Own property, manage your credit properly, and pay yourself first. These are the foundations of living a prosperous and healthy life. You should only use money as a tool to help you and others achieve your dreams. Remember, when it comes to wealth, it is not how much you make, but how much you keep. *(Money has never been my prime motivation. I've made some risky decisions in business matters, but I was careful to limit the impact of such decisions on my personal/family finances. I have always paid myself first. One of the keys to building wealth is to save consistently. You're better off saving $25.00 every payday than saving $100.00 three or four times a year. Practice being a consistent saver and you'll build wealth effortlessly.)*

11. Books

Expand your mind and learn about anything and everything through books and self-study. Reading can expand your world and make you smarter. One of the greatest gifts you can give to a child is to make reading fun. Never limit yourself. *(Growing up, I never showed any real interest in reading. I was a good reader but didn't enjoy it. My interest in reading began in college. My maturity level was such that I finally saw the value in reading. You can literally change your life overnight by reading a book.)*

12. Memories

As you grow older, memories become more important. Chronicle significant emotional events in your life, and refer back to them often. *(Most of my memories are positive. I don't have many negative memories. My positive memories have served as a blueprint for positive results.)*

13. Guilty Pleasures

Guilty pleasures—buying my first high-end luxury car, gambling in Las Vegas, spending lots of money for show tickets for my family—have led me to some of the best experiences I have ever had in my life. Make sure you have a few guilty pleasures on your journey to happiness.

14. Great Sex

The key to being a great lover is to feel loved. Sometimes another person can enter your life and highlight the emptiness in a relationship. If your partner can make you feel loved, then every moment becomes special. From the moment you make eye contact, to the embrace, to the smooth and gentle kiss—all of these are a prelude to great sex. The goal is to make the sex so good that your partner will be afraid to go to sleep for fear of losing that good feeling to a dream. You want your lover to want you every minute of the day. *(If you want your partner to know how you feel about her (or him), look your partner in the eye and say: "You have to know that I love you." If you say it and mean it, sex will be an emotional experience and not just an act of pleasure.)*

15. Teachable Moments

Look for opportunities to share what you know with others. For example, when your friends or relatives are feeling guilty about something, take a moment to remind them that guilt is a useless commodity. You can't eat it, spend it, or feel good because of having it. You can only manage those aspects of your life you truly have influence over. Forget about the rest of the stuff and move on. When you do share what you know, you will have exercised a "teachable moment." *(I've used "teachable moments" as a non-confrontational tool to educate people and change their lives.)*

16. Laughter

Laughter is universal and makes any day better. Scientific evidence suggests laughter is good for your heart, your health and your soul. Laugh as much as possible. *(I love laughter. I laugh as often as I can. I*

use laughter as a teaching and communication tool.
Change your life for the better and create opportuni-
ties to laugh.)

17. Courage

I define courage as the willingness to act on what you believe to be true. If you haven't had the opportunity to demonstrate courage in your life, you will. You will be tested in life, probably more than once. At some point, you will have to make difficult—and perhaps unpopular—decisions, but you will know in your heart that these decisions are the right ones. *(See sections on Pride and Faith.)*

18. Differential Treatment

Treat each individual differently. That's right. It's foolish to treat everyone the same. Deal with people from where they are and what they are instead of what you think they should be. The goal is to treat people fairly and equitably. If you are not sure how to treat them, simply ask them how they would like to be treated. *(I don't treat people the same. Everyone is different.)*

19. Friends

When I was about eight years old, my father told me, "Son, all you ever need in life is one good friend." Solid friendships are among the keys to a fulfilling life. Studies show that people with close friends have less stress in their lives, are more accomplished, are healthier, and will live longer. Need I say more? I've had the same group of friends for over thirty years. We talk several times a week, socialize consistently, and have never had one cross word. Friendships are one of the true joys in life.

20. Time

One of the keys to almost everything in life is to take your time. If you want to be a good lover, take your time. If you want to cook a great meal, take your time. If you want to lose weight the healthy way, take your time. Carefully think about how, when, and where you're spending your time. Having and using these options puts you on the road to success. Remember: "Slow and steady wins the race."

21. Forgiveness

Forgiveness is a gift to you. Healthy relationships cannot exist without forgiveness. There is no action so terrible that it can't be forgiven. The choice is yours. When you choose the path of forgiveness, you "free" yourself of anger, hurt, resentment and betrayal. Forgiveness allows you to heal and nourish your soul.

22. Pride

Self-pride is a direct measure of how you think about yourself. Behave in a manner affirming to you, and to others, that you are worthy. Doing and being your best is about character.

23. Being Nice

Being nice matters. Being able to say, "Please, thank you, you're welcome, excuse me, I'm sorry," and "May I help you?" will make you and everyone around you feel better.

24. Community

Get involved in your community. Share what you know and seek to make a difference. Such involvement is part of being a good citizen and a good neighbor. We need more "community-oriented" relationships in our lives. Get involved!

25. Acceptance

There are times in your life when you realize there are some things you will never understand. The best you can do is to accept that reality and move on.

Congratulations! You have completed the first step toward living a better life, today. You must make this list a part of your daily living before you move on to Step 2. Take your time. Do not rush the process. Make sure you have "mastered" *25 Things That <u>Really</u> Matter in Life* before moving forward.

STEP 2

STEP 2

25 Things That You
<u>Really</u>
Want To Do In Life

Now that you have integrated the *25 Things That <u>Really</u> Matter In Life* into your daily thinking, the next step is to list the 25 Things That You <u>Really</u> Want To Do In Life. This is a different list—things you *really want to do* before you leave this earth. The process of making a list is the beginning of a new chapter in your life. Do not limit yourself while making your list. The list will become your personal roadmap for living.

_____

_____

_____

_____

_____

_____

STEP 3

STEP 3

LIFE MASTERY
LIVING YOUR BEST LIFE

You are what you think you are. I believe every one of us has all of the necessary powers and gifts within us to live our lives to the fullest. Now that you feel better about yourself and are able to identify those inherent powers and gifts, you must use them! The beauty of *Life Mastery* is that you practice being good—and being good to yourself—every day. This allows you to develop yourself and become the "best possible you" for your family, your friends, and yourself.

Life Mastery is the way to cleanse your mind of all the dysfunctional thoughts that you've been having over the years. You didn't get that way overnight. You've had years of "cultural conditioning" and negative experiences that at times have led you to make bad choices and behave in a dysfunctional manner. All of the fault does not lie with you. Over time, when actions go unchallenged and unexamined, they seem normal. Thank goodness that's almost over!

Now that you know a lot more about yourself, you have more choices to help you manage and control the events in your life. It should also be clear that you—and only you—are ultimately responsible for your happiness. It takes more energy to live a lie than to live your life the way you know you should be living it. Incorporating *25 Things That Really Matter In Life* into your daily routine will allow you to live the life you want and to be the person you were really meant to be.

Life Mastery requires that you ask yourself, at the end of each day, one question: **What have I done to make myself proud?**

FINAL THOUGHTS

FINAL THOUGHTS

This book is your personal call to action! You're not reading this book by accident or chance. When you add positive energy in your life, your circumstances will improve. No matter how bad you believe your life to be, there is always someone who is in a worse position. You may think you have the worst job in the world. But if you quit your job tomorrow, fifty people will line up the next day to take that same job for less money.

My main reason for writing this book is to share the principles that have served me so well. You and I both know that life is full of high and low moments. Last year was probably the worst year of my life. I struggled through several personal and business challenges. When things got tough, I relied on the principles in this book and I always got positive results. In addition, my family, friends and the people I've met throughout my life have given me strength, courage and the will to fight my battles every day. I have so much to be thankful for. Many people tend to focus their energy on the challenging and painful areas of their lives rather than directing that energy toward the areas in their lives that are working well.

If you want to achieve success, you must consistently use these principles. I am living proof that you can teach yourself how to have positive thoughts. Negative thoughts can be minimized and, in some cases, eliminated from your mind. You have to trust the process, behave like a "recovering optimist," and think positive thoughts one day at a time. No one was born to fail. Everyone has the capacity to do and be something great.

STOP identifying with all of your problems! When you do this, you tend to see yourself as the problem and unknowingly work against yourself. Focus your energy on those things that are working for you.

By now you should realize that you are capable of creating your reality. By controlling your thoughts and emotions, you can create a collective positive energy that will follow you.

All you have to do is decide, in advance, that every day will be a good day. With practice, you will make every day a gift by focusing on the positive aspects of your life.

I wake up each day with a sense of purpose. I know I am capable of doing great things for myself and others.

Many people are searching for the "secret" to living a long and prosperous life. I'll tell you a secret: There *is* no secret to ensure good living and prosperity. I live by a simple formula that works for me: **I don't hate, I try not to worry, and I consistently give more and expect less.**

If you use this formula as your foundation and follow the principles in this book, you will be able to determine how to enrich your life and the lives of others every day.

Appendix

APPENDIX

IT'S TIME TO MOVE ON

1. How would you describe the quality of your life today and what would be your assessment of where you are in that life?

_____

_____

_____

_____

_____

_____

_____

_____

_____

_____

_____

2. Do you have any negative thoughts or barriers preventing you from living a better life? If so, list those that may get in your way.

_____

_____

_____

_____

_____

_____

_____

_____

_____

_____

_____

_____

_____

_____

_____

_____

_____

_____

_____

3. Review each item from the above list and identify what you need (such as additional time, more money, help from family and friends) to eliminate each barrier. Don't worry about whether you have the necessary resources at this time.

_____

_____

_____

_____

_____

_____

_____

_____

_____

_____

_____

_____

_____

_____

_____

_____

_____

APPENDIX

4. What are you most proud of in your life?

_____

_____

_____

_____

_____

_____

_____

_____

_____

_____

_____

_____

_____

_____

_____

_____

_____

_____

5. Are there any areas of your life that make you feel ashamed? Have you considered asking for professional help or turning to a "higher authority?"

_____

_____

_____

_____

_____

_____

_____

_____

_____

_____

_____

_____

_____

_____

_____

_____

_____

_____

_____

6. After reading *25 Things That <u>Really</u> Matter In Life,* I
have learned (or remembered) the following:

_____

_____

_____

_____

_____

_____

_____

_____

_____

_____

_____

_____

_____

_____

_____

_____

_____

_____

_____

APPENDIX

7. What is the personal and emotional cost of *not* living my best life?

_____

_____

_____

_____

_____

_____

_____

_____

_____

_____

_____

_____

_____

_____

_____

_____

_____

_____

APPENDIX

8. I will use what I have learned from reading and reflecting on the thoughts in this book in the following ways:

_____

_____

_____

_____

_____

_____

_____

_____

_____

_____

_____

_____

_____

_____

_____

_____

_____

Appendix

BONUS

BONUS

GARY'S RULES FOR LIVING

1. Most people are good people. Treat them as such until there is conclusive proof to the contrary.
2. Most people, if given the opportunity, will share something personal about themselves. Use this as an opportunity to make a positive connection with them.
3. We probably have more in common than we do differences.
4. Always give your best effort.
5. Be respectful! There's no excuse for disrespect. Ever!
6. Be polite.
7. The only difference between a good day and a bad day is your attitude. Attitude is everything!
8. Don't underestimate your personal power and sphere of influence. You <u>can</u> alter other people's reality.
9. Raise your personal standards for living (they are probably too low).
10. Ask questions when you don't understand.

11. Listen for clarity and strive to communicate effectively across lines of difference.
12. Deal with people from where they are, not from where you think they should be.
13. Perception is reality. Be careful not to discount someone else's reality.
14. Actively look for ways to include others.
15. Create opportunities where there are none.
16. Be a mentor – always look for opportunities to lift people up. It is your obligation.
17. Work hard to build TRUST (it will not happen overnight).
18. All you ever need in life is one good friend. If you have too many "friends," re-evaluate your circumstances.
19. Believe in yourself.
20. Sacrifice for your children.
21. Be honest with people. Give feedback for purposes of improvement and routinely praise and encourage others.
22. Be balanced and consistent in everything that you do.
23. "Same is not equal." Treat people fairly and equitably. To do that, you have to treat each individual differently.
24. It's not how you start in life. Rather, it's how you play the game and how you finish your life.
25. Pray and yield your burdens to a higher power.

ABOUT THE AUTHOR

A native of Washington, DC, Gary A. Johnson is the owner of the Gary A. Johnson Company, a management-training and consulting firm, and the founder and publisher of Black Men In America.com and Homework Help Page. com, two popular Web sites on the Internet.

Gary worked eighteen years for the federal government in a variety of positions including an assignment at The White House, where he worked on the staff for three Assistants to the President for National Security Affairs.

Gary learned how to use his personal power to define his success. The same personal power that we all have, but don't always know how to use—until now.

Want to learn more?

Visit the official 25 Things That _Really_ Matter In Life
web site at:
www.25ThingsThatReallyMatterInLife.com
or blog with us at:
www.25things.wordpress.com

Send comments to:

webmaster@garyjohnsoncompany.com

Learn more about Gary A. Johnson by visiting:

www.garyjohnsoncompany.com
www.blackmeninamerica.com

ATTENTION MEETING PLANNERS

To learn more about Gary's training seminars and consulting services visit www.garyjohnsoncompany.com Gary Johnson is available to serve as a **speaker, trainer** or **facilitator** for your organization.

25 Things That _Really_ Matter In Life: The Workshop

Harassment Prevention
Diversity
Live Your Dreams
Building Trust In The Workplace
Teambuilding
Respect In The Workplace

GAJ
Company
"Developing Leaders at Every Level"

LaVergne, TN USA
19 August 2009
155264LV00004B/28/P